Short Attention Span

Harry Guest

SHORT ATTENTION SPAN

Shearsman Books

First published in the United Kingdom in 2019 by
Shearsman Books
50 Westons Hill Drive
Emersons Green
BRISTOL
BS16 7DF

Shearsman Books Ltd Registered Office
30–31 St. James Place, Mangotsfield, Bristol BS16 9JB
(this address not for correspondence)

www.shearsman.com

ISBN 978-1-84861-687-5

CONTENTS

HAIKU

green, red or golden
leaves still flutter turning black
against summer skies

CORNWALL

Brown Willy climbed so long ago
broun wennyly in ancient Celtic means
hill of the swallows

DISILLUSION

A helicopter hovering around
a land of faërie at times believed
in, longed for anyway, has ruined thought
along a certain path uphill, alone,
those yaffle-taps heard on a nearby tree
unseen.

DEITY

the future of a rose, orang-utan or arsonist
the lasting of a shadow or a star
identify precisely all the colours of the sea
tell when exactly suns will disappear
and planets too
moons also

WHEN

There's only now, the past has vanished past
recall, to-morrow's unreliable
    as dreams, there's only now once more
        and now again and death
            what then

CHINESE GEOGRAPHY

There's a turtle that straddles the north
while a scarlet bird darts through the south.
When a dragon all blue roams the east
the white tiger's crossing the west.

ROTHKO

Lost on some lonely planet without hope.
Eternal night. Elsewhere there'd earlier been
colours of horizontal mystery
to hide or show this way that way although
not really present, left there not for glow.
Stretches of nowhere lacking stars froze time
for him for ever as he stood on grey,
one greyness, and no subtlety, self-death
thought of, not long to wait to cause the end.

ICELAND

a richer word ðan þankyou
    ðe þrill ðat þrobs þrough þoughtfully
    from þingvellir in state
    ðen standing on a glacier
        east of a waterfall

CONSTABLE

Sketch left on paper.
You almost see clouds ready
    to move, leaves stirring.

FEBRUARY

After the rainfall
two swans float on what was once
    a field gone blue now

AGE

My Japanese dissolves alas
    Like many other things –
Books, alkahest, nouns, veritas,
    Truths, mediæval kings.

Facts too: old remedies, short ways
    To go back whence I came,
Jokes, long division, titles, plays,
    Friends lost, that god-child's name.

PLATEN

Friend
there –
fair
end
they
told.

Old
play.

Nap
on
lap.

Breath
gone.

Death.

A sonnet written by August Graf von Platen on March 8th 1826 called
"Ich möchte, wenn ich sterbe…" (translated "in full" by Harry Guest in
Comparison & Conversions)

UNDERSTATEMENT

Some poets puffed by
too much praise may write drivel.
(It does get published.)

DUSK

Green evening. A block of flats
shuts out our sunset. Our house
darkens an apple orchard.
It isn't ours either.

ART

The painter takes a landscape as a scheme
for study, jettisons what would confuse,
moves trees and awkward boulders so they lose
the rôle they'd played and substitutes a dream.

LEE MUCH MISSED

A "difficult poet" called Harwood
Drank vodka the way any czar would –
        He went to his tailor,
        Said once "Hello, sailor!"
Then danced the hornpipe as a tar should.

SON

Nicholas at first, then Niko-san (for
Kugahara), Nichol in the U.S.
A. and Europe, finally then Nick who's
fifty now in Finchley, knows the cliffs though,
also Dartmoor, goes with me to Wagner,
likes gin with laughter and beats me at chess.

CATARACT

for Mo with love

return of colour gone
from reds to vision slowly pale,
lawns dimmer, autumn's leaves
less gold – all this
unnoticed passing by in decades,
                                        now
the sky's got back its blue,
its azures, sapphires, even clouds
at sunset fading in to glow

CLIFFWALK

the coalblack raptor I
imagined I have seen, blood on
each daisy and a sudden sea
that steams, one parable
of light, one padlocked dream,
juxtaposition of two shadows

FOR FOREIGNERS

In Japanese a haiku's not
three horizontal lines but runs
down vertically without a break
as if you saw a drift of rain-
drops glistening on a window-pane.

WHAT LISZT DID ONCE

let black and white fall
on a lake-sonata for
lovers to stroll by

2 A.M.

time for dreaming, time for terror,
intruder's footfall? how did who get in?
awake from nightmare where you'd left
cold claustrophobia squeezing out your breath

?

Quandary. Whether to. Or . . .
The first did have advantages.
Such as?

SONNET No. 18 BEGUN DIFFERENTLY

May I call you a radiant dawn in May?
That month seems less than charming, not as warm.
Winds rip frail blossoms for a sultry day.
Calm sunlifts can so often turn to storm.

SCHOOLMASTER

He taught you this, misunderstood that, changed
his torrid mind from one day to the next
aside a consequence which made no sense

LASSITUDE

They're at the frontier again.
                              Really?
The selfsame lot, well-armed.
                              A yawn.
Those ones who know we're still
outnumbered.
                    Sighs heard.
                                    You know
they're ready to advance.
                              Yes
but who cares? Who cares?

ISLAND

waves flecked with spindrift
long silhouette of dark rock
sky one haze of stars

                                        —Bashô

THE SEVENTH ONE (*i.e. No. VII*)

Our next king (Welsh, living en France)
must have been lazy since the maid
would wake him crossly with a loud
"Réveille-toi, Henri! Tu dors!"

LE NAVIRE NIGHT
après Marguerite Duras

They never met but loved by telephone
ferried by darkness with a ship not there
kept from each other by herself who died
just having married someone else not loved

CYNICISM

There's a dark streak in everyone, a sin
that's nourished year by decade, prejudice
lurking behind each friendly tolerance

SCHOOLING TO-DAY

yoga and meditation won't
work quite as well as playing right wing
and (briefly) for the second eleven
also running up the Malverns
so sweaty breathless as you pass
to centre half or reach the top

POLITICS

Should antidisestablishmentarianism
and floccinancinihilipilification
(the action or habit of estimating as worthless)
increase in Llanfairpwllgwyngyllgogerychwyrndrobwllllantysil-
      iogogogoch *
without the necessary Lichtwellenfortpflanzungbewegung-
      geschwindigkeit **
as well as Rhiw or Ayr or Eye
something has to be done

A village in Anglesey
** *The speed of movement in the reproduction of light waves (a feminine noun)*

WARNING

The truth's too hard for poetry to grasp.
Reality's too slippery to catch
the look of loving, force of violins,
precise curl of a once there flower, that cold
    walk one November down a street
        you had not known
           was there

SHADOWS

though clumsy, arms about each other, up
the moonlit avenue to after months
of doubt will one? the other? daring to
assume each would expect the same response

THE FINAL VERSE

Why does this coffin seem to you
    So weighty and so wide?
I took my love, my sorrow too,
    And placed them both inside.

           (from Heine's Lyrisches Intermezzo)

SESTOS, EARLY MORNING

She stumbled over something on the sand,
turned round surprised, reached down
to shift some seaweed, found
the drowned eyes of Leander look at her
unseeing

UNPLEASANT TRUTH

Not knowing how to catch the swaying of
a poplar makes a poet pause, rethink
et cetera. Not like the painter.

CHILD

    she slipped into sleep (sometimes)
    like an otter on the river-bank
    leaving hardly a ripple
    on the placid surface of the water

THEN

when colours pack their bags and echoes can
    no longer get through cobwebs then
a sun breaks past in time to grieve again
    as tears on grass far sadder than
drops from a statue's melancholy eyes
prove nature also has her alibis,
feels love, despair, shame, happiness
                              …ah, when

WHAT HAIKUS ARE

    streaks of slow lightning
twisting the once obvious
    to something different

BORDERS

The sea Ruled lines of rollers
        One incessant hiss
Walk inland to find silence

DEATH

It sometimes starts with little things.
A cough. A cut that won't quite heal.
A patch of ineffectual rash.
Conclusion can of course come soon
or drawn out agonisingly
but always gets there in the end,
the unknown end, the inescapable.

morning

it's ten past eight / i might as well get up /
i've dreamed enough / forgotten some / now yawn /
remembered kisses / not regretted them /
perhaps i should have one or two / that's far
too late to worry / there's no need to taint
the quotas of a very lucky past

DRINK

Three days each week I make my choice
of whiskies, vodkas, wines, liqueurs,
port, sherry. The four other ones
stay dry – unless of course a friend
invites us over for a glass
or more. It would be churlish to
refuse though my dear wife has fixed
a calendar of temperance.

F. CHOPIN. *PRÉLUDES Op. 28, No. 20*

Three dirges sure and confident despite
their minor key fade further one by one
away as though receding to admit
a wronging till the last one for the last
four bars lifts like an echo back to pride
        then sighs to find finality
                guides quietude once more
                        into a star –
                                less night

FLAT EARTH, ETC.

The sun's an orb. Seeing a pale
disc beyond scurrying clouds he
turns away finding it hard
to disbelieve the astronomers

IN WINTER IN ESSEX IN 1959

We took to sodomising more
and more, alternately, in bed
or standing up, twice on the floor.
One chilly evening he said
we're wasting time and stopped the car.
He did me, I him, in a field.
What bliss! Watched by an icy star
to give and take, vanquish then yield.

POETRY IN SCHOOLS

The Times keeps mentioning *leading poets*. Who
are they? Who are they leading where? And why?
In any generation there are few
real poets who can challenge, mystify
and thrill with grace and convolution. All
these scribblers who condemn learning by heart
must fear their "work" lacks lasting value. Call
their bluff. Make lazy teachers make kids start
to roll rich words around the tongue, explore
strange worlds and find what poetry is for.

84

My head's of lead. I stumble as I walk,
forget words known each time I stop to talk,
stare bleakly, dumb, feel I'm once more a bore
who grins insanely waiting frozen for
a helpful hint from her or him to break
the ice and name the gap brought by heartache.

NO ANSWER

the thrill of disobedience then
a cube of darkness round you like
a room, some guilt preferred. What did
I do to earn such loneliness?

CARE

words won't do it nor
windowfuls of what
you thought you'd never
wish to buy and help
them out for once so
cautious rather think
again pragmatic
is perhaps the word

MEXICO

"zaman hujan au"
(long moment of the ash rain)
close by volcanoes

WITH THE CONCLUSION OVER

Will I then never after death-throes be
a me again? No past remembered? Wife,
the children, friends, jobs, gardens? Failure? Be
a scarecrow placed somewhere, ignored? Or will
another kind of me be made to climb
once more from babyhood, shed glories with
the dross and trudge along the rota of
a new unfolding life just to, well what

IN GRATEFUL MEMORY OF BOB NASH

You taught me tints I'd never seen and how
to feel closed images, hear lost sounds in
a place you somehow turned from nowhere to
a somewhere as you often did where then
I learned to edge my way more fruitfully
and bathe in light you'd brought which made me move
enticingly a little nearer to
the many other things you'd seen, recalled,
loved, understood, explained and always shared

NIGHT CATS

One sleeps demurely while the other groans
and sometimes quivers in a dream display
of movement done next day or weeks ago

WHEN THOUGH

I have no alibi.
Since everyone must die
one day (I won't know why)
I'll have to say good-bye
to all that's nice and try
to fly up to the sky
perhaps though fall to fry
where Satan's said to lie
in wait for thugs who spy
on those that terrify
the world, make us all cry
"What will disqualify
the stubborn or the wry?"

CHOICE

                not bleak
oblique and beautiful
that music slanted against the text
sunlight and the blue music of the waves
distant singing

A CERTAIN DAUGHTER

A beautiful lady called Tasha
Is never bored, dull, slick or brash. A
      Delight, (how I miss her!)
      An artist, such bliss, a
Bright star every way. What a smasher!

WHAT BAUDELAIRE IMPLIED

hope vanishes tears fall
the only sound are sobs
while that atrocious anguish like
a despot plants its midnight temporary flag
on his bowed skull

(Miss Dickinson however wrote "*I felt a Funeral in my Brain*")
The second edition of Les Fleurs du mal, *containing Spleen 4 came out in*
1861. Emily Dickinson's Poem No. 280 was possibly written the same year.

WINTER

                    beneath
         the hazed blue sky
         in late December
         one slim daffodil
         like a yellow-cold
         poker braves the frost
         on neighbouring blades
         of grass

QUESTIONABLE

One slash of rainbow to the north
its imitator further out
with fainted colours from the shower
                    Both fade away
The transience has won once more
(but these are only facts and facts
were rarely poetry)

A PAIR IN LOVE UNKNOWN ALONE

Two lithe boys who had an erection
Stood naked to watch their reflection
    They said "We're not failures!"
    Then grabbed genitalias
And tossed them both off with perfection.

DOVES

   X̲ one da dá
z   X̲ one da dá
z   X̲ one da dá
z
(*sometimes there is no final "z"*)

      or to put it another way

     I'm not mournful
oh   I'm not mournful
no   I'm   not mournful
but

3 A.M.

    evil thoughts wrap round
    me in the small hours
    pretending the grey's
    not orange this time

RUBÁIYÁT

There cannot be
a noose of light
because dawn's blaze
comes from the east
leaving the west
a shadowed half
which will become
at dusk a blaze
the east by then
left in the dark

BIRDS

A cardinal flashed into the ivy
cloaking the house across the way.
In vain I waited for him to re-appear.
We left next day.

#

That young beech swayed in the wind.
A dozen sparrows chattering
swarmed at the tree,
leaving the sky empty.

#

The summit reached past nine.
Black rocks among the snow.
Twelve thousand feet. One raven
cawing at the sun.

CONSOLATIONS

Some foliage seen further or
how lakes hold half-moons glittering.
From time to time at work I saw
snow-flurries come and go. A lane
that leads to somewhere could still bring
dreams of a distance under rain

EAST OF WHERE

In Devon-speaking "*Yes*" means "*East*".
The highest point in England's south
of Cumbria is called Yes Tor
because it's east of somewhere there.

BIRTHS

All different. I arrived on southern Wales;
my wife quite near the Mississippi; then
our daughter on the coast of Sussex; son
in the Far East, the furthest of Japan.
Two rivers (one the Severn), Channel and
Pacific Ocean. Four with water by.
Does that mean on the edge of things or not?

LOVELY COMPANIONS

To some extent the winter turning back
    looks chilled, forlorn yet from
   the kitchen window choice of greens
around plus tanned leaves stay stuck to the ground.

   No roses in the narrowness
of our conservatory five pink geraniums
  ignore the twilight and accept the dark

APRIL DUSK

When rhododendrons fend the twilight off
azaleas burn like sulphur and the last
camellias fall full-petalled to the earth
all tints are quenched soon by the Paschal moon
remembering the kiss that gave the kiss
away and lit three dangling corpses for
three nights to make their pallor graver till
they're dead for certain ready for the graves

ABSENCE

The moon is late tonight, there's something wrong.
It should be seen by now behind
the pear-tree stripped of leaves
this autumn only visible
each evening from the bathroom in
the elongated night time when
no clouds are acting like a veil

TASHA'S COLOURED PHOTO

in Cotentin, south-west of Cherbourg

Long triangle of foliage, one-
sixth of the picture. To the right
a line of trees. Sky mostly, with thin clouds.
So peaceful.
           Only nature.
                      Look closer, for
behind in distance, tiny, hard to find, a
silhouette: Mt-St-Michel

www.ingramcontent.com/pod-product-compliance
Lightning Source LLC
Chambersburg PA
CBHW021949040426
42448CB00008B/1311